**primitive
cartography**

**primitive
cartography**
paul summers

STACK
BOOKS

Smokestack Books
PO Box 408, Middlesbrough TS5 6WA
e-mail: info@smokestack-books.co.uk
www.smokestack-books.co.uk

primitive cartography

First published by Walleah Press, Tasmania, Australia, 2013

Cover image: Ian Stephenson, Sfumato (1963-5)
© the estate of Ian Stephenson.
Special thanks for Kate and Steve Stephenson
for permission to reproduce this painting.
Author photo: Keith Pattison

ISBN 978-0-9575747-9-3

Smokestack Books is represented
by Inpress Ltd

for ash,
ryan & aaron

contents

dasein

a primitive cartography

anaximander of miletus
is gazing at his navel.

herding a world of sepia
lines within the confines

of a single leaf. a genesis
from the nib of a crow-

feather quill. the things
we own or think we own

now mapped into an order
of convex arc & steadfast

poles; an ocean abstruse,
three continents adrift:

just rapture & despair,
between them longing.

gossamer

wellington point, queensland

a boy in wisconsin
has murdered his father.

a single round to the back
of his head. here, on the point,

the lizard is spared;
the kookaburra retreats.

sanctuary in the shadows
of the eaves' cool silence.

an old hibiscus is heavy
with bud; her spastic leaves

fit in the drip of flesh-warm
rain. a fly-wing fragility;

the moment contented
in its own sparse company.

healing o'malley

emu park, central queensland

hunch-backed, the threat-less clouds
advance, in rank, to stoic obsoletion.

the haze of landfall curdling to a form,
a darkness as viscous as drying blood;

& blue upon relentless blue, the heavens
dig in, securing their dome of holy vantage.

o'malley sucks an oyster from the grip of its shell,
gratitude drowned out by the crackle of his lungs;

his prayers fragmenting into fever's tongues,
encrypted laments for her grey-faced votives.

coowonga stalks bream in the jade's convection,
still as a crane & sapling lean; haloed by the morning

glare. the saviour's skin aglow like jet; aglow like love,
for want of better, every lumen both simple & brilliant.

new year's day

the stars align, a clock will chime;
the year of the bereaved, again.

the year of the perplexed, of blank
denials; unanswerable queries on

faith & justice. hamstrung by the
mystery of your sudden departure.

we dredge a case of ritual wine but time
still drags its callous feet. & rescued

again by glowing dawn, the left behind,
we scour the beach for extant cures.

the ghost of your ashes on the sand
cementing our losses. the tide is liable,

the moon complicit; delivering drifts
of straggling diaspora: drowned petals

& beer-tins, the space-craft bulges of
a putrefying stingray; whose pleas are

gagged by a barricade of maggots,
whose eyes are egg-yolks washed

with hot butter. intrigued by the reek
of natural death, the youngest boy

dissects a concept with the blade of his
tongue. the eldest is quiet, squat on his

haunches & fingering the sand; feeling
it spill through the cracks of his grip.

skin

just as she begins to speak, a blade
of molten light lays down to bleach

an airless veranda's feathered teak.
the first for weeks to breach this cage

of crooked laths. beneath the tongues
of drooling palms, a flemish flake of brass-

necked snake unwinds itself to hunt
the warmth. her sheath of scales made

shabby by the moult of growth, the chore
of metamorphosis. i hear the hiss of her

cris de coeur; the ache of her costume
nipping at the ribs. a snake in her prime

abandoning her skin, shaking it off
like the gesture of belonging.

the covenant of grace

the language of this sunlight
has moved beyond beauty;

both star & the shadow
silenced by their brilliance.

& truth has learnt to hold
its tongue or see it ripped

out by inquisitor's follies.
let the day define itself;

watch it choke on clumsy
words. let it learn frailty;

like a child finding grace
in the covenant of petals,

like the cuckoo finding love
in a breath of stifled kinship.

tab

all heads are bowed
in the church of the fallen.

a drowning swell of hope,
the curse of possibility.

marty's dad has the skin
of a corpse, lumps the last

of his pension on another
stable whisper. a muddling

pace & trapped on the rails.
the jockey looks vexed,

two sweating handfuls
of leather & weight.

he comes home like a train
but they exit defeated.

lazarus

two boys on the beach
are re-enacting history

white-man versus savage
a foregone conclusion

imaginary muskets
& imaginary spears

powder-flash & thud
relentlessly they die

then rise like lazarus
to make their war again

in a cell near wee waa
a murri boy is beaten

a dampened blanket
pulled over his head

cupboard love

stuart feeds the birds:
a ball of mince, a ribbon

of ham, a grub unearthed
whilst thinning out his ferns.

a dialogue of mimicked calls,
a word of encouragement.

today, he is muted by
the weight of his losses.

the birds still come; heads
cocked & beaks bowed.

un-noted in my pocket-
book of australian birds,

the magpie's capacity
for demonstrative care.

crunch

i.m. jimmy oates

we are spinning for plump mackerel
on the pier at south harbour, a flash
of scarce sunshine in a summer of grey
making auras of the fuzz of our awkward
pubescence, igniting the chrome of those
hand-me-down bikes. our lures flickering

like short-lived dreams. we are sharing
smiles, the weeping segments of a flesh
warm jaffa. time dissolves in jumpy edits;
a crash-zoom cliché: the newlywed wife,
the tragic accident, the helpless brakes
& screeching flames. her empty young

widower, in painful succession, a whining
old honda at break-neck speed, a tractor
in stasis, straddling a junction. no need for
a note of sorry explanation. the weight of
your love compounding the impact, the
groan of losses in the crunch of hot metal.

luncheon

a fifth dan in denial, i fashion security
from a knowledge of indigenous flora;

each name catalogued & filed, the latin,
& colloquial. & fauna too: the idiot bat,

the ubiquitous rat, the club-footed quoll
who squats in our roof void; each of them

lacking in landing gear protocol, they break
our sleep with their slap-stick misjudgement.

let's not mention the venomous snakes.
i lunch alone, except for birdsong & ants,

except for the trees & a vast asthmatic ocean,
a distilled frangipani which masks my musk.

i watch the clock from half past two, awaiting
the onslaught of your raucous inquiries.

easter

today, the sun
makes calvary

of an island's hump
haloed & austere

poised for theatre
expecting cameras

a retired country doctor
whose skull is full of mahler

& untouchable nurses
calmly gives the kiss of life

to a woman on the road
who's still & grey outside iga

a neglected bougainvillea
is scourging blue air

kiss

tonight, within this slab of sauna heat we sprawl
like flattened toads on grass as warm as breath
& eat. we feed each other wide-hipped prawns
from bamboo bowls hand-crafted by the children
of xi'an province. our fingers taste of brine & lime,
the sickly syrup of over-ripe mangoes. we hungrily
kiss, devour our feast & then each other's burning
skin. the beer we drink will cool our lips. we have

grown adept in silences & in naming constellations,
have learnt humility from the weight of their light. we
have conjured a sunrise in far-off darkness; launched
prayers into this dome of sky & sung; each fragile note
or lyric swarm like billiard balls they kiss the glow of the
southern cross, a careful trajectory guiding them home.

grandpa's hands

& being, as they were, in
the arse-end of nowhere

he stitched the gash
with 5lb monofilament,

a barbless hook
& long-nosed pliers;

some belated utility
to that night-class

in upholstery.
each sheared-off cell

cowering like tallow
from the reach of flame.

a spinal ridge of straining skin,
the punctuated seep of blood.

the price of coal

that night when we cried
half lost in the half-light

of the umpteenth schooner
& extravagant sambucas

we put it down to catholic stuff
the trauma of collapsing roofs

rare questions comrade, & raw,
& rarer still in this state of men

who rip up rock in search of gold
both reasoned & reflected on

how long before a child might
losetheir grip on trust & love?

how long to unlearn the warmth of
breath in daddy's goodnight kisses?

the blade & the lamb

i

through a glass less dark

dr. o'brien dreams of utopia,
shortly after midnight mass,
christmas 1899

he imagines it different:
the miner's bones uncrushed,
the shrill of a still-birth's hungry scream,
a punch-drunk boxer's flawless recall,

the red-faced squatocracy disposed
of their gout & their ornate gate-posts,
the syphilitic curse undone,
the judas cow absolved of guilt,

the mountain unbroken,
the river untamed, the poor un-poor,
the black-gin leaps un-thought,
hatred unfed, our hearts intact,

our morning-after lips
still capable of welcome.

ii

tiocfaidh ár lá

dr. o'brien dreams of home,
st. patrick's day, 1916, rockhampton

barefoot in the slurry
of an awkward amputation

he is conjuring wolfe tone
from the mists of innisfree

his rhetoric un-gilded,
his wounds un-healed,

reflected in the blackness
of a properly-pulled pint

the docile heather holds its breath
a cataract of dampness is clearing

from the bog-side, hibernia's blank
borders are there for the taking

a devil's dominion imprinted on
the brim of an orange-man's hat

iii

broken

dr. o'brien contemplates defeat,
saint kieran's day, 1917, rockhampton

the strike is broken;
so too the blood-line

of this issueless soul.
the railwaymen return

to work, their forelocks
bowed & tickets marked.

my blade exhumes a dead-
man's spleen. the flesh grows

cold upon the slab. this cancer's
grip too deep & fierce to conjure

any victory. no cure or elixir.
we falter, the faithful, toward

the schism. all fight expended, all
vigour defunct. thy will be done.

iv

our father

*dr. o'brien converses with his god,
on the assumption of the blessed
virgin mary, 1929, rockhampton*

forgive us our trespass,
the folly of our longing.

look kindly on the grieving
& the huddled poor;

the shoeless & subordinate,
the muted & enraged.

forgive us our doubt,
the burden of our vanity.

let the sisters on the hill
remember compassion,

replenish their hearts
with ubiquitous mercy;

a flourish of grace
foreclosing all else.

v

arrival

dr. o'brien pronounces a death,
new year's day, 1945, rockhampton.

a dozen slow years
perfecting his losses

his head full of graves:
their molehill mounds

of sanguine soil & futile
blooms, precarious cairns

of smooth diluvia,solidity
hanging on their kissing

parabola. a life of foxed
pages as fragile as blossom.

with gentle thumbs
i draw his ruffled

eyelids shut; as peaceful
now as any arrival.

fitzroy triptych

i

genesis /a second coming

a flimsy brig throws shadows
to the sepia depths. her lines
secured in straining knots on
hanging trees along the bank.
the forestays hum a broken
hymn. the boatswain gnaws
his gilded pipe. europa's germ
decanting her cargo of spurious
progress; her clutter & rank,
the pains of labour, the syphilitic
cell. the fish look on, the eels
perplexed, the dragonflies
take to the wing; a sentence
suspended in a dome of blue.

toonooba blues

the brewer's stack lets loose a belch
of lawless steam; the aura of a sacred
god ascendant from spumescent mash.

the wharfies swarm & derricks strain,
the town-gas men in sulphurous toil.
the noon-day canon sounds too soon,

rouses a cormorant's basking wings;
the snake-neck tar sends fingerlings
like phosphor sparks into the weed.

the crabs commence another dance,
each limb on point, each fitful step
bequeaths the tide a clouded ghost.

toonooba sings her whispered blues;
the herons bow their heads in prayer.

iii

ingot

the wharf alive;
a brackish fug
of sweat & curse,
of lanolin & amber
rum. a *barra* leaps;

each lustred scale
a flake of light.
each tail-blade flap
a leaf unfurled from
some drowned book.

a swansong kiss
for advent air;
a gloss of salt
upon her lips.

swansong triptych

i.m. anna pavlova & the winter garden theatre, rockhampton.

i

entrée

la reine des oiseaux
est en train de mourir.

trapped in the dust
of crumbling wings

the conch shell hiss
of corporeal applause

mimicking the crackle
of her bubbling lungs.

wheel out the strings,
their stalwart adagio,

plucking the chambers
of our feathered hearts.

bring me my costume.
bring me the swan.

ii

le cygne

luminous, her spectral limbs
entice the air to take her hand.

each fluid reach, each fragile pointe,
a breath to sculpt a slumping nape.

elevé, glissé, bourrée suivi,
la tombé dernier.

the rise, the glide,
the falter & the fall.

aplomb gracieux.
all movement translation.

the queen of bird's reluctant soul
escapes the clutch of exquisite lines

learns new steps from anoxic ghosts:
the cadence of loss, the art of dying.

iii

coda

trapped in the dust
of these lifeless wings

a choir of mutes
takes breath & sings

obscured by the weave
of saccharin strings.

the weeds reclaim
this defunct stage:

*rambling dock
& angel's hair,*

each tendril flex
an avant-garde

to colonise this
dirt with grace.

blackbird singing

scouring the blue
for eureka's cloth-stars

a swallow soars;
elusive as solace

in the steady void
of exile. a fragile song

set free on the breath
of mizpah prayers.

all hope enslaved,
despair unbound,

each day between
indentured poles;

we shine the floors
you dance upon.

uncle bob dreams of victory

rock-vegas goes to war

a ruthless prussian draws a line in the dirt
urbana to asheville, novitskaya to biak
daubs of black blood dragged through
the contours of the papuan heat
from buna to hollandia, to hell & back

a vain triumvirate of gilded stars
illuminates the faces of the mustered dead
illuminates the cheek-bone of his dear miss em
the white linen flags of her quiet breaths
merging with the fug of smoke & bourbon

& a nightingale sings on eichelberger square
a rank of tagged corpses all deaf to her melody
an angel absconds from heaven's swelled arc
to pin another medal on the flatness of his chest

cut

peak downs surface mine, qld

drought-gaunt
& mourning shrill,

the bell-bird tolls,
a muted threnodial.

brittle boned,
the hapless shale

surrenders all vantage
to dragged incisions.

our mark is made,
the grave is cut;

this crumbling bund
a crick-neck bolster.

& obdurate, a stoic sky
throws down its blue.

neuropathway 61 revisited

we are nothing more than a gallon of water
& a cupful of salts; a few trace elements,
absorbed through osmosis from our lavish
environs: some lime-scale & rust, a coke-spoon
scoop of alienated longing, a smear of petro-
chemicals, a knob of lard. elements more infinite
than unmapped stars. a pinch of turmeric to
authenticate our jaundice, a dab of glucose at
once recast as sculpted lumps within our throats.
we are brambling in the dew of yorkie's farm,
the gas-yard wall & beanley's ringses. the drunken
unevenness of pudding chare. the smell of your hair.
the ishmailova snow & las ramblas springs, the breath-
warm rain on the graves of pere la chaise, a fuchsia

in bloom or blackbird's song, a slick of sun or bloodless
moon upon an ocean that is not mine, a cloud, a tree,
the taste of blood, the dance of these shadow's brief
encounters. perhaps there'll be a touch more lard, a crumb
of flaking pastry, a smudge of ash, the rendered blubber
of the slaughtered lamb. we are nothing but energy &
calls to action, a fleet of memories adrift in the humours.
they swerve the chicanes of a glowing web of dendrites;
despite all efforts some collisions are inevitable. we are
nothing but miraculous, each pathway & each map-less
route kissed into life by you. by you & you. we are nothing
but cells of light & dark, of colour made concrete through
our own illumination. we are nothing but equations of
love & hate. we are nothing now but a ghost of ourselves.

the acquisition of knowledge

3 festive biscuit tins; each square & robust.
2 dickensian christmases in primary colours,
1, an obese robin perching on the bailey of
an overturned pot & each imbued with silent
snow; nicotine stained & rusting, his mis-spelt
name scratched in triplicate in a spidery gothic
font; the effort of each letter, a shallow dent
laid down for posterity. a hundred eggs, all set
like jewels. sixty species & assorted swaps. the
sweetness of sawdust & nature's fragility. once,
before we all grew bored with birds, he swapped
fat stephen a tidy clutch for only one. goldcrest
& redstart, kittiwake & dunnock, linnet & long-eared
owl, all for the privilege of a hard to get merlin.

dew point

i check the forecast
every day, meticulous

as prayer. a communion
through weather. so very,

very english. the parabolae
of hemispheres, a fleeting

kiss of straining arcs. i imagine
youin the garden, trenching

the potato patch, opening
up that thick, black earth,

your stubborn, old bones
creaking like a schooner,

excited for & expectant
of the year's first frost.

ascension

emu park, qld

& today's archipelago
a confident abstraction

a stuttering stroke
of japanese ink

telegraphy transcribed
on the arc of distance

a muted ascension
through the mercury's jig

the she-oaks preen
their flaccid manes

a sandbar melts
in modernity's promise

these gulls swear allegiance
to this fleeting republic

strange days

three men are on the roof, replacing
sheets of rusted tin. the ghost of a radio

escaping the huddle of another muted
smoko. sad-songs & bad news, an advert

for shoes made cheaply in china. an eagle
drops a snake-head at my feet, neatly

severed & appearing to smile. it must mean
something. it would to you, with your love

of crystals & penchant for tarot. ouroboros
slain. this cycle at an end. & on another day,

within another draft, another version of this
vain psychology, it might to me too. a little

less empirically left, or on the shelf, still
coldly enlightened but open to magic.

parklife

the lads have found a friend:
a murri boy with matching specs

whose carer is consumed by
a pressing text. we watch them

play, oblivious to difference,
oblivious of all language,

the weight of hatreds, the burden
of their privilege. they make a ring

of roses; their little, sweaty hands
entwined in knots. a phosphor burst

of joyous promise, both effortless
& short-lived, like that crackle of light

as drought parched dirt sucks in
the gloss of a season's first rain.

mute

today's discovery is less than welcome
a quiet mass within your womb, a smudge
of pure colour on an ultrasound scan. dense
& lifeless (they hope) & passion-fruit sized.
they talk to us of calmness, & conservative
approaches. how softly, softly the angels will
tread. & the darkness has hardened into a fist
& your bow-taut nerves to undoable knots.

the moon is blue & almost full. & heaven's arc
a glitter trail of hopeful stars, titanium white.
a frog-mouthed owl, both mute & still, stands sentry
on the ridge-cap of a hot tin roof. we are trading
half-smiles in the silences of evening. we are
watching the sky for a change in the weather.

hurt

last night i dreamt of johnny cash
fingers raking the scuffed *bon aqua*

every raw verse molasses & gravel
every terse chord a broken dream

he stood alone, his eyes aglow with rage
& love, acetylene arcs in the pilbeam's fog

a room of steaming men looked on in awe
nuggets in their throats & brackish tears

the ghosted communicants moving as one:
the Fitzroy dockers & the barcaldine boys,

the railwaymen & the lake creek crew; the oil
& blood of honest toil still wedged beneath

their fingernails. i wear this black for the working
class. i am here tonight to honour your perdition.

breached

a hand-span away
from my shadow's end

the ants dismantle
a dying cockroach.

their flickering mania
lapsing time. an eye,

a jagged curve of jaw
a leg, a wing, a plate

of armour, breached.
the metronomic grass

is rocking in its trauma.
no better hour than this

to ponder impermanence;
no better foil to vanity's spell.

mirage

shelley beach, emu park

today, the heat haze
makes islands weightless;
a convoy of basalt
defying gravity,
their footings breached
by a trick of light.

tyler scours the rocks
for crabs & words
to free his palsied tongue;
each quarry elusive,
they dart for the cover
of immoveable stones.

the slow surf sighs & glassy
eyed, the curlews mourn.

keening

today, the ocean is torn
between anger & repose
a bubbling simmer
of banded jade

the islands recline,
their conscience cleansed
by bleaching light

two vain gulls skate
the mirror of wet sand
a turtle corpse on the rocks
jaws loosened by death

this sky is history now
all time subservient
to the weight of our losses

low point

it's strictly need to know.
a heritage framed
in pub-quiz wisdom.
a red-letter logic
transcribed in the oracle
of our *tally-ho* papers;
imprinted on the lids
of our ice-cold stubbies.
the precise time & date
of bradman's every century.
australia is home to more
than 500 species of reptile.
the monolith formerly
known as ayers rock
is over 8kms in circumference.
lake eyre, in drought,
is the country's lowest point.
an absence of genocide,
or evolving apartheid,
the stolen generation,
the gestural reparation,
the lame charades
of ownership & rights,
the rape of the land,
a witness-list of profiteers,
the ice-cold statistics
of adolescent suicide,
the ice-cold welcome
of narou's canvas ghetto.
lake eyre, in drought,
is the country's lowest point.
a hollowness brimming
with the opposite of laughter.

cartography

the ocean is docile
the day unconscious

lulled by the dullness
of the unreflective

the shadows perfect
their primitive maps

old valerie waves
she has a new hat

a need for voices
other than her own

she busies herself
with the puzzle of grief

the orchid is pot-bound
strangled by boundaries

not 'babe'

elastic, the hours dig in
their stubborn heels.

the litter, a maggot-mass
engulfing weeping teats.

& the runt is dying,
septic & deserted;

each slumping capillary
an unwinnable skirmish.

a shallowing of breath,
that poisoned charge,

a fatal avant-garde
who've lost their ranks:

grown cruelly imprecise
in search of an ending.

mapping the abstract

the air is alive
a thistle-down intrigue

the thermals raise
their gossamer flags

the swallows stitch
this gaping blue

a silent dance
of predator & prey

the filigree cloud
reflects on impermanence

the ferocity of this light
the depth of its shadows

each moment re-mapped
to fragile abstraction

the return of the loons

for kenojuak ashevak

the night they come
this dark acquires

a fatal wound & so
they mourn. a narrow

blade of hissing phosphor,
a blister growing ripe

on the arc of distance.
they are diving again

for unclaimed votives,
drawn back to the void

by a flicker of silver.
an ocean, bereaved,

her skin of black water
seeking out light.

bert hinkler's fear of mountains

you are gliding through the vistas
of a child's recurring nightmare.

the stick is cleft, your feathers
clipped. you teach him the fear

of a powerless decent, the twin-
edged blades of surety & risk,

each virtue rendered lame
by the fickleness of thermals.

& the angels are grounded
by a vacillating heaven,

a brutal clot of avoidable rock
thrown up into the blue.

il duce is weeping by your broken frame;
blood on the laurels he crowns you with.

sonnet 98 (or thereabouts)

emu park, central queensland.

the labial mauve
of vernal dawn.

the islands breach:
a smudged ellipsis,

a history extant,
obtuse & unsolvable.

the sea almonds blush,
embraced by drought;

their cockatoo gloss
of soot & blood aglow

like every doubt to grip
this season's frailties.

we hear the downy ferns
unfurl & turn a deaf ear.

interregnum

zilzie, qld

& awkward in their transience
the shadows bristle

shrinking like philosophy
to the root of their existence

the gutters drip
with crushed vanilla

the basalt poised
for future's inquiry

as blank & immoveable
as our fear of departure

a fragile interregnum
of sunlight & rain

the swallows recanting
the puzzle of exile

postdiluvial

zilzie, central queensland

today, these waves a swill
of milky tealeft too-long
stewed. a glowing bruise
of agitated crows which
grows in haemorrhage over
by the boat-ramp. the body
of a cow, displaced, framed
in a clichéof cartoon death:
a lolling tongue, the skyward
legs, each pipe distended &
ripe to pop. a drift-linecordon
of wilting macramé, a slick of vain
tributes, of wild hibiscus torn from
the plain of some drowned valley.

protocol

dawn has the sheen
of a golden bird.

2 geckos dance,
their jazz-hand

antics oblivious
to the protocol;

their gormless joy
enveloped in a slick

of rain-tree musk
& sweating mulch.

they see off the dregs
of denim night, slope-off,

to colonise the silence
of a dead man's shoes.

flinch

today, the waves
are curdled blood

washed from the hands
of some distant dictator.

the pine trees flinch,
the anorexic palms

convulse, a tangle
of recoiling fronds,

disgusted by the curve
of dysmorphic limbs.

the islands look on
blind to all atrocity

this light exposing
their guiltless grins

brother wolf chokes on his tongue

i.m. barry macsweeney

let us drink again then,
to the prison of his days,

to a dead man's wardrobe,
praise-less & now emptied,

to the stench of torment,
& the undiscovered dead,

to all our infidelities, drink,
the strong & the untameable.

let us drink & drink,
make void the ghosts

of laughter, the dented
& unloved, of hearts

as dark & marbled grey
as piaf's sorry gravestone.

fin

& humbled again
by the weight of stars,
we salvage ourspoils
in cardboard boxes.

an album spills.
an avalanche mosaic
of art-school stills
prostrated on the dirt.

& see us, there,
in black & white,
as confident as lichen
in our bit-part beauty.

our eyes complicit,
my teeth intact,
your crocheted beret
a web of intrigue.

& warm as breath,
the shrink-wrap night
is coaxing an end-theme
from reticent cicadas.

thought for today

exquisite mojitos
& shrinking ice-caps;
but mainly the mojitos,
to be perfectly honest.

the sun's long fingers
on the hump of my posture,
the docile ocean's lisping choral,
a palm quartet's kendoka adagio.

& reflected complicity
is raping our comfort;
clouding this moment
like lime clouds the rum.

do polar bears crave blankness?
does weeping jesus pine for home?

scorch

cawarral, central queensland

blue tongued, the flames
re-stake their claim

a flourish of rekindled dead
whose whispers haunt

the hiss of amber steam
the dry-boned groan

of the charcoal's contortion
the scorch of land & lung

the stoic gums succumb
their shadows melting

into cold perdition
a continent's guilt

reduced again to memory
all solidity to fragile ash

mate

beneath a brutal sun that bakes my stooping
neck as red as yours, we scratch at the surface

with blunted spades, barely disturbing this fired
crust, this scab of heavy ochre grown concrete

& inglorious in years of drought. the futile marks
we make as shallow as our mateship or the truth

of our histories; neither art or labour, they will not
stand a test of time, an inch of summer rain will see

them gone; this thankless earth returned to grace.
& still you will cherish your calloused hands as proof

of worth; your currency of briny sweat not love
or idle words, not tenderness or grief. beneath this

block of queensland sky let dogma fly, let fathers kiss
their sons & cry or bid them forever a fond goodbye.

cane toad fella

i will cleanse this garden
of their poisoned genes;

exorcise this dirt of ghosts
& still they will come & still

repulsion lends itself to fuel
the rigours of this, my ritual:

a cricket bat or any stump,
a golf club or a paling lath,

anything hands can be laid upon,
any means to stamp this order:

a bullet, an axe, a blackgin leap,
a simple germ or quart of grog,

the cover of darkness, the veil of history,
anything to do the job, to do the deed.

creek

yeppoon, central queensland

a neat phalange of mangrove pods
pierces the dullness of muted silt;

like arrows of fortune awaiting flight,
their heads immersed in acts of survival.

cicada drone, the wing-beat leatherette
of auburn bats, the slow hiss of drying

stones, the finger-snap of startled crabs,
all sound dissolving in the element's flux.

shark-eyed, the breakers lick the fudge
of sultry dusk, a lunar cadence on the fur

of their tongues. they probe the pewter
sand for truth, melting the evidence of all

previous tenure. the fisherman hurls his
baited hook; hope invested in every cast.

valentine

cicadas fall silent, lulled to comfort
by whispered dusk. the moon

deployed; a quarter formed. we dance
on the breath of an ocean's slow music;

a gentle tangle of torso & limb. insatiable
mosquitoes unite our blood. the possums

look stoned, grinning & gormless, imagining
these hapless bats as terriers in gimp suits,

as gothic houdinis suspended in swansong.
we dance on & laugh, our breath enveloped

in the night's slow music: the parched palm
quartet's *kendōka* adagio, the tongue-tied

surf in her lisping celebration, a parliament
of our smiling ghosts negotiating dowries.

like paint drying

her blood forms a skin
on the kitchen's scuffed

lino. the perfume familiar:
the reek of exertion,

the rum on his breath,
the bristle of a rage

kept barely under wraps.
a storm-bird is singing,

its mournful agitation
unravelling the jewellery

of the city's cold light.
her sisters share a cigarette

at the hospital gates.déjà
vu. they wait for news.

stet

snared in a tangle
of contrite kisses

choking on bubbles
of the other's breath

& every frisson
elatory as light

each clash of teeth
a clumsy erratum

the blushing digits
the flush of living

he pledges a version
of something like love

& just for once,
she lets it stand

they say

when darknesses collide
a stippled light, newborn

& weak illuminates another
space, another distant place,

where things are nameless,
not even things for want

of language, each entity
a void, as lonesome as

a widowed swan,
they hold their tongues

or things, like tongues,
for want of language,

rehearsing their roles;
awaiting their moment.

historical society

when the speed lab went up
we made it onto *abc*. 3 full

pages of full-colour photos splayed
across *the bulletin* like some royal visit

the golden flames licking the sunset
the dragon breath of the overcooked

& her, the mother, a frantic silhouette
caught in the glare of stop-frame terror

she is dragging her baby from a smoking cot
her clothes & hair & skin an ugly dance of fire

like kim phuc emerging through the napalm heat
like those monks in tibet enacting silent protests

every vile scream judged & filed, catalogued
now & put away; marked *not for exhibition*.

the kings of sorrow

the drizzle strips
the palette bare,

as blank & as fragile
as methuselah's hair.

the kings of sorrow
face down the waves

& stare, their weary
eyes relinquish care;

like gods invoked
in the white-lead

glare of a guiltless
sun on contrite air.

all history drowned out
by the cackle of seasons.

shallow water

north stradbroke island, queensland.

another fat bream ploughs a lazy furrow, mouthing a barrage
of silent profanity. sinking sun spearing the arc of her flank

every scale, the fresh sheen of shaved pewter. enter right,
the shadow-play shark's deadly geometry slaloming weed,

riding the barrel of an outstretched wave, the distance between us
well flighted spit & fused in the weld of fear & awe, exhale, incite

the breaking surf to dissipate the blood-scent on my hands, transform
the pasty bow of english legs to mangrove root, the tautness of my
spastic

trunk into a trunk. i shaman, shallow water shape-shifter, shark-
whisperer, deceiver of the squalus, order of the lucky bastard, the fool

who fished at amity, at dusk, in water made murky by the mud-crabs'
dance; what privilege this, to meet your killer in a dream & be awake.

haven

christmas island, december 2010

heavy now as ballast lead, a weightless
baby drifts from vision. wide-eyed but

lifeless, melting in the twilight of expanding
depth. she waves in the drag of undertow &

saturated lungs. each gilded globe of fleeing
breath seeks refuge in the cusp of sky & sea.

each fragile bauble of misplaced hope exploded
in the tensions of a rolling swell. & heavy now

as ballast lead, their empty hearts grow cold
& dead. all dreams defunct in waking terror.

they melt into expanding depth. their muted
eyes accuse, though lacking any focus; they fix

like cadavers on points of consensus, their pupils
pulled like moths towards the light upon the hill.

siren

the islands advance;
drawn by the pull
of your open mouth.
their crop of doubts
ripening like blisters.

a spine of brittle cloud,
each straining vertebrae
stretched to dislocation:
the yank of time, the surge
of wind, the idling gravitas

of sluggish sun. & the gulls
are redeemed in a paradox
of thermals. this light has made
us kings of all that we survey.

anzac day

i am dividing agapanthus
in the midday heat
tender work, teasing
apart their conjoined roots

a juvenile butcher bird
has ventured indoors
scavenging the crumbs
of our breakfast debris

a baby is wailing
across the paddock
the idle wheeze of sea
unravelling in the treetops

i am watching the ants
retrieving their dead

we're going on a crab hunt

for aaron

he is learning the perils of juvenile oysters,
the unrelenting rigor of neptune's scalpels;

his fingers unusable for more than a week.
his scars acquired in the name of inquiry;

in the name of blue swimmers & half a dozen
shrimps, to be precise. the devil's in the detail.

& discovery always nestles in the darkest place;
always seeks the sanctuary of weightiest rocks.

thrice a day, religiously, i dress the lines of oozing
stigmata. & tearful but stoical & quietly proud, we

strategise our next incursion. the sepsis has receded;
red & systematic, retreating with the grace of a proof-

reader's biro. a niggling pain in the pull of new skin,
the contraction of cells, the slow act of reparation.

for judith fellows

whose cells conspired
to cut her short

dead in her prime
& someone else's

i finger these photos
like morphine phials

both welcome & not
like midnight's ghosts

they grind the edges
of these angled days

a million miles now
from splendid youth

& all of our promise
dissolving into fact.

slouch

zilzie, central queensland

today, each cloud-bloom
has the weight of debt;

perching like doubt
on a skein of islands.

sickle-winged the swallows
slash the monotone of lapis air,

unravelling the mysteries
of the beaches' archaeology.

the slouching basalt basks
on parched-mouthed grass

& the sea is shrinking
like my mother's pale limbs;

leaving rock-pools to perfect
the ambivalence of longing.

blood

rockhampton, central queensland

the moon discloses her blushing
misdemeanours; deep cadmium,
vermillion hue, as red as this dirt
& unpaid bills; the necks on which
those porcine heads stand propped.

imprinted like the ghost of an angry
hand, whose digit span will dissipate
to curfew flush; a subconjunctival
haemorrhage; an egg-yolk blighted
by its foetal growth. & the black boy

with petrol eyes is sharing his injustice
with a copper's deaf alsatian; cuffed &
prone, hidden from this sanguine light;
adrift again up the shittiest of creeks.

hamstrung

there are ghosts
in the safety glass,

obese & smile-less,
& vaguely familiar;

trapped like fossils
in cages of nostalgia.

choking on nuggets
of lethargic vowels,

a brood of pale biddies
moan about weather,

a toddler is hamstrung
by the weight of a nappy;

& somewhere between
them, an irreparable union.

biblical

once there was a word
& that word was love

blooming like a rose
that could not last

once he found a pair
of bloated blue legs

kicking through seaweed
on hendon's black beach

once he beat a man
within a lesion of death

for raising a hand
to his sister's sweet face

a fury with the weight
of a lead crystal ash-tray

the shipping forecast

today, trees lean west.
duck the gale's frenetic

punches. their subjugate
fronds whipping the grey.

& fragile gulls toil, all
their flight now stasis.

here, ships sing dirges.
each dour note extolling

the toll of tangled surf.
prospero, oh prospero!

the islands are greyscale.
pelican & *hummocky*,

the blur of *wedge*;
a vanishing act.

il museo dell'oumo

the *walker's* shortbread tin of carefully pinned moths,
a work in progress, the *texaco* '74 world cup coin set,
missing number 11, the beer-mats & the stamps, neither
sustainable, the 1:72 scale luftwaffe fighters minus the
prototype jets. the *tsb* gonks which had aggravated his
asthma. the fragmented clay pipes, the ticket stubs &
the comics, the almost entire back-catalogue of early
clash singles on 7 inch coloured vinyl, the fading *polaroids*
of nameless girls at soulless parties, his father's 1936 first
edition of lenin's collected works in twelve pristine volumes
but missing number 11. two grown-up sons & an arthritic
labrador, his wife estranged & recently remarried. a whole
slow life plagued by the almost, a whole slow life to learn
of absence; the archivist's curse of incomplete collections.

the etymology of hockle

bebside, northumberland

the dogs of memory need a feed.this reek
of hair oil & stale *old spice* excites in them
a hunger. once, in the gloaming of that tarry
shed, i watched you splicing two flax ropes,
each daughterless plait pulled roughly taut,
all tension maintained in sure-handed magic,

your ancient art applied by rote, by touch & grip
& quiet strength. their union was invisible. ours
has grown knotted in the *rolleywaymen*'s secrets.
beneath an elder the ground ferments. imprinted
on the bristles of an easter hoar, a trace of fox, of
corn-mouse & dainty roe, each legacy twice under-

scored by theslow-worm's dull adventures. a single
primrose is poised for song, a doily constellation of
cow-parsley florets, each frozen web a cable-length
now threaded with glass beads. the sun looks down
upon your gifts: a smile within a look of loss, a hand
within a hand, a wordless trek through dock & nettle,

a faith in hope, the philosophy of senses, a sprawling
nose & cave-man brow, this posture & these words. the
etymology of hockle; our vernacular vulgar for stringy
spit, that bursts its core in flight like worked-outrope,
each tendon frayed & trod upon, in need of reparation.
your chapel has become a forge, your old stone school

abandoned. a museum piece, preserved behind bars
& a masque of surveillance. the only sign of progress
here, a blistered skin of tarmac to shroud the cinder-
path. each bulging window's imprecise, etched with grit
& smeared with oil. i place my open hand, palm-down,
against the pane & watch my warmth create a ghost.

a case of you (gap year)

emu park, central queensland

a strange place, this, you'd think, to find
a lassie from kilmarnock the worse the wear

for drink. not an obvious habitat, you'd think,
for fear & loathing, for pain & denial spawned

in the weave of these grey, bereaved carpets.
the pokies crave attention; their disco-light grins

& fruitless rainbows. she is standing now but prone
& quite alone. lost in the strobe of their premonitions.

her fragile voice is beautiful, both honey & peat,
like oban whisky, or *gregory's girl*, or even home

a hundred wee frogs, she said she'd kissed
an' no' one of tha cunts turned intae a prince.

& i just smile & gently nod, strike my most empathic pose;
i draw a map of purgatory, her face sketched on it twice.

twelfth night

gaza, january 2009

no star over bethlehem;
only the phosphorous
bloom of hate ingrained
like mould into the night.

a lexicon of twisted steel,
of fractured brick & concrete
mauled, of shard & splinter,
of burnt hair & rendered fat,

the ferric reek of blood;
of gunshot & silenced babies,
of shoe, of limb, of broken cup,
of limp dead growing cold,

dusted with a halo
of this spiteful dirt.

slant

emu park, central queensland

the arse-end of a cyclone makes the rain perpendicular;
as steady as drizzle but amplified in volume in a straight
correlation with the scale of this land-mass. tight & jaded
as the weave of harris tweed, the cross-hatch of its mesh
is almost impregnable. & the news will be bad; it always is:
mr svendsen's prize-winning brahman will tragically drown,
wrapped in the bulge of a brackish creek. the fat, unsmiling
banks-man who plies his ruddy scowl at the road-works
by the slaughterhouse will tragically contract trench-foot
& aggravate the wheeze of his nascent emphysema. a whole
pallid legion of anaemic earth-worms will tragically drown,
evicted from their home in anoxic loam. i will wash my feet
in the flume of a down-pipe. & sour-faced, the swallows stare,
they skulk & sulk behind the steadfast drip of flaking eaves.

fall

wing-beat & caw
the fleeting blur

of shrapnel crows
disrupts the blue.

a silt of blossom
swollen to a drift

like muted snow.
the sun still shines.

the shadows spill
their graphite slicks,

even the clouds
are warm as milk.

the seasons' cusp
a forfeit estate.

barcaldine

the tree is dead; long blighted by some liberal spore,
knowledge spurned, the fruit has withered on the vine,
proud banners shelved; stakanovic become a whore.

red-faced lawyers at the bar, serpents rotten to the core.
the shearer's sweat is cold, rusted blades refuse to shine,
the tree is dead; long blighted by some liberal spore.

an idle union grows obese; abandoning esprit de corps,
the light upon the hill is black, our number in decline;
proud banners shelved; stakanovic become a whore.

eureka's magic moment lost & chronos slams the door,
our hope confined within the oubliette of every mine,
the tree is dead; long blighted by some liberal spore.

at barcaldine, a war is won & lost, our wounds still raw,
solidity has melted into air, our rhetoric into a whine,
proud banners shelved; stakanovic become a whore.

now in defeat, & drink, we'll mourn for then, before;
raise a glass to all this rotten ghost gum can enshrine.
the tree is dead; long blighted by some liberal spore.
proud banners shelved; stakanovic become a whore.

elymus repens

couch grass

in d-day raids, not talked about, he'd earned a *dsm* & *bar*;
he'd never cried or to this day once sat inside a german car.

& now, every sunday, instead of chapel's thankless chairs
or tedious broadsheet news, of which he despairs, he wages

ignominious war, in shock & awe, upon the very grass on
which he walks or sometimes kneels in mumbling prayer;

a self-penned penitent who barters for redemption. let buyer
beware. futility is a concept lost on him. he rips at the rhizomes

probing his borders. no inch given; attention to order. stiff & cold,
his digits rake, they strafe across diluvial loam, frozen in a trigger

poise. he routs out the shoots of this couched malignance, madly
clawing at the breathless soil. *twitch* or *scutch*, call it what you like;

all language spawned in the tangle of our bloody roots; the stubborn
dendrites knotted in our heads. he will not, or cannot, let nature win.

flirting with the buddha

another year & still no messiah;
enough signs now, you'd presume,

with the hindsight of enlightenment,
in the awkward silences of millennia,

in the cold, closed-off body language
of these moulded polyurethane deities.

faith's bland alchemy has rendered its change:
passion to compassion & water into wine,

commune to communion & dust to dust.
perhaps it's time to fix this mess ourselves?

i'll suggest hammers, you prefer mirrors,
the dull catharsis of reading groups or *nlp*,

i'll favour fast-track divorce. you prefer some time apart.
this time tomorrow you'll be flirting with the buddha.

glare

main beach, emu park

the sky is a kiss
of sprawling blues

a huddle of frail cloud
formulates intent

skating like swallows
on the bulge of heaven

the rapid surf spits
her liquid dance

a cubist cormorant
warms his wings

the day melting in
phosphorous glare

our histories dissolving
in a rhapsody of shells

commemorative

beneath these ranks of gallipoli pine
we gorged ourselves on cake & wine
dispensed of all precept, let every line
be blank or better still as free as time
pale virgins in a tango of cello curves
a knotted sheath of frisson nerves

oblivious in our matinee of peacock youth,
our hungry tongues too busy (or too wise)
to probe the moment's grace for any truth
the weight of our kisses averting our eyes
to the transit of the seasons & passer-bys
who deemed our passion unholy or unwise

the days grow old & left behind; they grow
more fragile than our grip on faith, our love
anonymous in this haemorrhage of shadow,
more fragile than my grip on faith, my love.

labour day

go tender comrades
keep raised our flag

though gorged today
on feasts of losses

re-cast the mallet
grind the blade

& from the dust
of fractured time

re-sculpt our pledge
in words so bold

that fragile gods
on gilded clouds

will tremble
bearing witness

homily

rocky point, emu park

we are sat on the lap
of the tie-dyed tides.

teaching our children
the language of turtles

polite & economic
but laden with simile

then once perfected
the etiquette of terns

whose pristine lines
this sun makes concrete

& later, we'll examine
the grace of the oyster

humble in its silence
but scalpel sharp

ouroboros

woorabinda, central queensland

beware the magi bearing gifts;
their votive grog & lavish guilt.

the former, laced; the latter,
the spike. shame & the shame

of shame. death & the death of
death. the snake will bite its tail;

& these mothers, their tongues.
a silence forged, a flawless edge

to hamstring progress. the birds
have flown. the kangaroos have

seen the light. the brumby bolted
to the downs. three score years &

ten of drought & flame, of blood &
shit congealing on this bitter earth.

the tailor of coalburn

this ancient dene, enclosed by act of law, still bears our name,
though title's lost. your sons & theirs would scratch its toughened
skin for troves of coal; their future sewn up in midnight indentures,
in cross-road pacts on bewick moor; each shift of sun or starry sky
relinquished for their daily bread, for salty broth & quenching ale.
from magic to modern in seamless transition. all mystery denied
them, they lurched toward perdition. resistant to the magnet pull
of change, your stubbornness grew concrete; you perched yourself
in waxy light reluctant still to give it up, your journeyman's craft
laid out in antecedence. your bale of cloth unrolled, an ocean
weave in trough & swell, but every fault is ironed flat or brushed
aside. & you are poised with chalk & shears, with every pattern
in your head, each line by rote; a collar to grip the squire's throat,
a cuff to take his lady's hand, to robe your golden age of want.

the records show you took to making sails; moved east towards
the german sea. each seam relearned in treble-stitch, each dart
& eyelet with the promise of transit. five sheets to the wind, you
dreamed each pregnant canvas arc robust & swollen in a tempest
gust, each curve voluptuous as rising dough, as the heaving breasts
of courting doves. today, two centuries or so away, a hemisphere
between us; i am mending my children's fallen hems, repatriating
school-shirts with liberated buttons. within this cell of queensland
heat, i tack & hitch a running-stitch; each ligature hapless, my hands
unskilled at all but gesture, my genes cut baggy & low-slung; muscles
devoid of harboured memory. & every clumsy prick of skin has freed
a globe of velvet blood; i stem the flow with lips & tongue, savouring
the warmth of a muted communion, the taste of passion's salt & ore,
& each endeavour borne in the art of a northern collier's bulging sails.